MILITARY SERVICE

A WAY TO SUCCEED

By

David Ferrier

With

John Mandala

BATTLE PRESS

Battle Press
SATELLITE BEACH, FLORIDA

AFTER YOUR MILITARY SERVICE
A Way To Succeed

Copyright © 2021 by David Ferrier.

Battle Press books may be ordered through booksellers or by contacting:

Battle Press
1-919-218-4039
steve@battlepress.media
www.battlepress.media

ISBN: 978-1-7378-2382-7 (softcover)
ISBN: 978-1-7378-2382-4 (eBook)

Library of Congress Control Number:
2021918303

First Edition

Personal Information

You can enter your personal information here, if you like, in case of any emergency or accident.

Name:

_____

Address:

_____

_____

_____

Phone #:

_____

Emergency Contact:

Name:

_____

Phone #:

_____

Thanks

The author wishes to sincerely thank those individuals who have supported this important endeavor and to all those who have served in our nation's armed forces.

A special thanks to my friend, John Mandala, who provided the template and inspiration for this project.

Table of Contents

INTRODUCTION 7

PREFACE 11

CHAPTER 1 Where, When, & How to Begin 13

CHAPTER 2 How to Get Your Needed Documents........... 17

CHAPTER 3 Transition Preparation 30

CHAPTER 4 Getting on the Web & Where & Why 35

CHAPTER 5 An Example Discharge Program 39

INTERLUDE I The Greatest and The Most 46

INTERLUDE II Holding onto Positive Energy (HOPE) 49

BEGINNING OF PART II 52

CHAPTER 6 Preparing for the First Day 53

CHAPTER 7 Finances & Living Well 58

CHAPTER 8 Some Words on Employment 61

CHAPTER 9 Service organizations 68

CHAPTER 10 HOME SWEET HOME 72

CHAPTER 11 Conclusion 75

APPENDIX A Cover Letter, Resume, Job Application, & References.. 76

APPENDIX B Work Search Record 86

APPENDIX C Resources.. 88

Here Are Some Words of Wisdom:

The willingness with which our young people are likely to serve in any war, no matter how justified, shall be directly proportional to how they perceive Veterans of earlier wars were treated and appreciated by their nation.

-President George Washington

America has many glories. The last one she would wish to surrender is the glory of the men who have served her in war. While such devotion lives, the nation is secure. Whatever dangers may threaten from within or without, she can view them calmly. Turning to her veterans she can say: These are our defenders. They are invincible. In them is our safety.

-President Calvin Coolidge

It's about how we treat our veterans every single day of the year. It's about making sure that they have the care they need and the benefits that they have earned when they came home. It's about serving all of you as well as you've served the United States of America.

-President Barrack Obama

INTRODUCTION

Every year, approximately 200,000 men and women are discharged from military service. Less than 50% of these veterans will use their GI Bill Educational benefits and less than 50% of those who do will receive a degree. This is a waste, a tragic waste of an invaluable resource, a life changing tool.

Fewer than 12% of veterans will use their VA home loan benefit and only 10% of all home loans are VA loans. Another waste.

DON'T BE JUST ANOTHER STATISTIC! DO SOMETHING WITH YOUR LIFE!

A majority of freshly discharged veterans are unemployed, if only temporarily. The federal government and most local and state governments give priorities to hiring veterans. Many businesses receive tax considerations for the numbers of veterans they hire. Not taking advantage of this consideration is a waste, another waste of your hard-earned benefits.

Any honorably discharged veteran seeking employment has a far better chance of finding work than even a college graduate if they apply their military skills and education in the proper workplace. This guidelet is about how to get started doing that, as well as how a veteran can obtain the health, educational and financial benefits he, or she, earned by their military service.

It is the hope of the author that through the distribution and use of this planner, that men and women will increase their chances of successful transition to civilian life. This guidelet is packed with information you will need to ease your transition back into society. Use it well. Let's get started.

FIRST STEPS

Your discharge from the military is the beginning of the rest of your life. The training and experience you gained in the military can be a substantial factor in making your civilian career a success. And you have earned LOTS of help from service organizations to make it so.

Use this guidelet/planner, contact your service agencies, follow their advice but always **personally and independently manage and oversee your life's direction**. You have learned, through your military service, that Freedom is not Free. Neither is Success. You have a lot of help coming to you, none of it will be of any use if you do not learn to help yourself.

You have probably been to a series of pre-discharge lectures before your separation. "Death by Power Point" is how I have heard them described.

Mountains of info, overwhelming facts and figures, well intentioned, but all easily forgotten in the rush back to civilian life.

This guidelet, *After Your Military Service, A Way To Succeed*, is simple to follow, to the point, and won't burden you with so much information that your attention span will be taxed.

We are not going to give you hundreds of addresses to look into, we're not going to preach, and we're not going to baby you. We are going to point you in the right direction and then the rest is up to you.

We are also assuming that you have set yourself up with a place to stay upon discharge. For the vast majority, "Home Sweet Home" is the answer. Your parent's home. Your childhood home.

> ### *KEEPING IT SIMPLE IS THE KEY TO EVERYTHING! IF YOU KEEP YOUR LIFE SIMPLE, THEN NOTHING CAN COMPLICATE IT!*

You are no longer a child. You are an honorably discharged United States Armed Forces Veteran. Time to take down the Star Wars posters and start thinking about getting a place of your own. This, of course, could take some time. Home is a great place to start. It is not necessarily a great final destination. This guidelet will help you get ready to live independently, find a job, get needed documents in order, and give you a place to store your information and personal history. It will help you pace yourself and provide a "pit stop" at times to measure your progress in becoming a progressive, self-sufficient person.

Read this guidelet and
get started!
Remember, every day, no matter
how overwhelming it might seem, is
still the first day of the rest of your
life. Make it count.

WE WILL NOT BE JUDGED BY THE
PURITY OF OUR ACTIONS, BUT BY THE
INTEGRITY OF OUR COMPROMISES.

BILL WEBER

PREFACE

Military service builds soldiers through discipline, character, responsibility, training and trust. All of these virtues and tools will be indispensable to you in charting your post-service future. If others (employers, family, friends) are to recognize these qualities in you, you must first recognize and personify these virtues to yourself.

America needs workers. America needs leaders. You have demonstrated both of these qualities while in the military. Now you must convert them. For your sake and your countries.

You have already been trained to get up, get ready and productively use the day. Your military background demonstrates that. In many ways your transition to success in the civilian world is very

> **THE CREATIVE SPIRIT IS THE MOST UNTAPPED SOURCE OF ENERGY IN THE UNIVERSE.**

much like your habits of success in the military. Rise early. Clean yourself. Lay out your uniform for the day. Tank tops and cargo shorts are not the costumes of the successful job seeker. Just as you did in the military, dress appropriately. A collared shirt and a tie are never a bad idea. Eat a good breakfast, have a plan, get out of the house and GO.

Use these skills, these habits in your civilian life. These will place you miles ahead of your competition.

Many job seekers spend hours trolling the internet for opportunities. On line is a great place to start but, just as in the military, **BOOTS ON THE GROUND** is going to be the ultimate step in finding work.

To assist you in your job search: **Appendix A** contains a sample cover letter, resume, job application form, and a place to list your references. **Appendix B** is a work search record to list potential employer's names and contact information. Do not wait for them to contact you. Give it a few days, continue your job search, then go back and contact them. Follow up, follow through. Be responsible and consistent. **Appendix C** includes a list of valuable resources you can use to ease your transition back into civilian life. Also, there are several blank pages at the back of the guidelet to list your thoughts, strategies, and other information and have it all in one place for easy reference.

This guidelet is not simply to read, it is meant to be *used*. There are spaces you can fill in with information you will need before or upon discharge. You can begin to use it *now*, so you can continue to use it as a planner, reminder, and data source.

CHAPTER 1
Where, When, & How to Begin

Most veterans believe that once they are discharged they will begin dealing with reentry into society. This is a fallacy – Wise people will tell you that preparations for civilian life should begin as soon as you have decided you are not going to make the military your career and have a parting date set in your mind.

Every soldier knows the exact date on which they will be discharged, barring any unforeseen consequences, such as a disciplinary action resulting in loss of enlistment time. Your ETS, (Expiration, Term of Service) is set in stone, a date guaranteed by your enlistment contract. If you do not plan on making the military your career

> **START PLANNING NOW.**

(reenlisting), NOW is the time to start your post-service plan.

Incidentally there is generally a three year window after separation from the military when you can reenlist without necessarily losing rank or having to repeat basic training. These conditions are negotiable with the recruitment service of your chosen branch of the military however, and exceptions, pro and con will be made. You should talk with a recruiter as soon after your service discharge as possible if you are considering reenlisting in the Armed Forces.

Time and time again, behavior in the military is a clear-cut insight into whether a person will be successful upon discharge or will soon fail. Did you choose a Military Occupational Specialty with specific, transferable applications to civilian employment? Have you taken advantage of voluntary training programs which would enhance these skills? Have you explored available educational correspondence courses from outside the military? It's never too late to get started, it is up to you.

VETERAN:

It's not that I CAN, And others CAN'T.

It's that I DID, And others DIDN"T.

Begin now by filling in the dates below to remind yourself, the goals you have are the goals you will achieve.

SET EMPLOYMENT DATE

_____

Six months before your earliest discharge date is an ideal time to begin preparing and using this guidelet and planner. However there is no bad time to get started. You have this guidelet NOW, get started NOW.

SMART PEOPLE LEARN FROM THE MISTAKES THEY MAKE, WISE PEOPLE LEARN FROM THE MISTAKES OF OTHERS.

The following is a simple checklist for you to begin the process of preparing for civilian life. You will be surprised at how many things you can mark off your list in no time at all. Moreover, it will give you a "visual hope" and confidence that you are moving in the right direction towards your successful transition into society.

A List of Discharge Needs

These are the things you should have before or upon discharge. Check these off as you obtain them:

_____ Address Book / Phone Number Lists
_____ Birth Certificate
_____ Budget Plan
_____ Certificates / Degrees
_____ Credit Report
_____ DD-214 Military Papers
_____ Driver's License & DMV Record Review
_____ Medical Records
_____ Medication List
_____ Resource List
_____ Resume
_____ Short / Long-Term Goals & Plan
_____ Social Security Card
_____ Time Management Plan
_____ Computer / Internet Access

If you are struggling with a substance abuse, you should also have the following:

_____ Inpatient / Outpatient programs in your area
_____ List of nearby 12-Step meeting places
_____ Social / Support Groups you will be attending

CHAPTER 2
How to Get Your Needed Documents

Address Book – Everyone should have an address and phone number book to keep their vital addresses and phone numbers handy. It can be a small memo pad or a nice leather-bound, line-paper book you might spend some money for at a stationary store. If you attend A.A. or N.A. meetings, it is good to have a book with phone numbers you can call if you are having a problem with something. Get one or use a separate piece of paper or a pad if necessary.

Birth Certificate – It is important to have a copy of your Birth Certificate. If you did not get it while in the service, you can get it by writing to your local Department of Health.

Budget Plan – When you get a job and begin to make a paycheck or even if you already have some money saved upon discharge, it is a good idea to have a budget plan. Determine your costs of living for the week, which will include food, housing, transportation, clothing, and any other expense you might have for that week and add it up. Deduct that from your pay for that week, and make sure you have enough left over in case of an unforeseen circumstance, like a car breakdown that needs to be repaired. When you get settled and start making regular paychecks, make sure that your food, rent (if any), utilities (gas and electricity), and any car insurance or other critical bill is paid right off the top.

These monthly bills are going to be in your budget plan permanently, unless you move, or something changes in your monthly living expenses. Be sure that you set up a budget plan that allows you to save for these monthly payments out of your weekly or bi-weekly check and pay them first, leaving enough for food and clothing.

Tip: Paying your bills using direct deposit from your bank account is very helpful to make sure they are paid on time and you don't incur late charges.

Credit Report – In this day and age, it is vital that you obtain a credit report for yourself. There have been instances where unsuspecting people have had others use their Social Security numbers, obtained illegally, to get credit cards and buy things without paying for them. If this has happened to you,

you will never know unless you get a credit report on yourself.

The three major reporting centers you can call to obtain their mail-in forms or get your credit report on-line are:

EQUIFAX – 1-800-685-1111 or
www.equifax.com
TRANSUNION – 1-877-322-8228 or
www.transunion.com
EXPERIAN – 1-888-397-3742 or
www.experian.com

Be alert to changes in your credit reports. Some-one else may be using your Social Security number or credit card number to make purchases that you will pay for in the end!

Tip: You can contact each credit reporting agency once per year, so if you spread out your requests for a credit report to one of these agencies every four months, you can always have an updated report for yourself. This will help you quickly find out about someone who might be using your credit for fraudulent purposes.

DD-214 (Military Service Records) –

Since you served in the military, you should have a copy of your service record. If you have not obtained one before discharge, you can normally go to a local recruiting center and they will give you the form to fill out to get your records. On the form, it will direct you to the address where you'll need to send the form to get the required record, since it's different if you were in the Army, Navy, Air Force, Marines, or other branches of the military. <u>When you receive your DD-214 MAKE LOTS OF COPIES</u>. Always leave a copy of your DD-214 with your job application. Due diligence.

Driver's License – Every state has a Department

of Motor Vehicles (DMV). They will be able to provide you with a printed record of any unpaid tickets or suspensions on your license. To find out about your license status, write to the state Department of Motor Vehicles where you obtained that license and ask for an abstract. Once you receive the abstract, you can begin to consider what steps you need to take to clear up any outstanding tickets or determine what will need to be done to restore your license to a valid status. If you do not have a license, and never had one, you will need to go to your local DMV office to determine what types of ID you will need, and what steps you'll need to take to get a license. Remember this: You can look up your local DMV in the phone book or on the web.

Medical Records: – If you are taking any type of medication or have any health problems, you should request copies of your medical records. You have a right to obtain the copies of your medical records but it is critical that you have these so that if you see a physician on the outside, you can give them to him or her and it will save them a lot of time on your case. To obtain records from a specific hospital you may have been treated at, you will need to get the address of that hospital and write to them.

Medication List - This goes hand in hand with getting your medical records. If you take medications, especially crucial ones like HIV meds or blood pressure meds, always make a list of them and keep it with you. If anything happens to you, doctors will be able to take steps to make sure you are not given anything that will cause an adverse reaction to other medications you may be taking.

If you are diabetic or have serious health issues, look into getting a Medic-Alert bracelet, which will make it even easier for doctors to quickly determine your needs if you are unable to communicate with them.

Job Search / Employment Plan - You should set up for yourself a daily planner, which is described in Chapter 5 & Chapter 6 in this guidelet that you can follow on a daily and/or monthly basis. Without a plan, you are basically lost when you are discharged. Make one now!

Employment history - You should always have a copy of your employment history, particularly if you have worked prior to the military. A steady, relevant employment history from a young age demonstrates initiative, reliability and character. List not just the jobs but any job references, with contact information, you may have. References count a lot.

Describe, in your own words, the skills and training necessary for you to have held these positions. Describe not just the technical aspects of what you've done but the inter-personal skills that were necessary to do your job. For example, if you worked at a fast food counter before you went into the military describe the customer skills necessary to get through a shift. Did you handle money? Lock up or secure the premises?

Whenever possible contact and ask for letters of reference from former employers. Keep copies with you, leave them with potential employers. Explain why you left each prior position you have held. Self-betterment, higher pay, more potential are always good explanations.

Sit down and make a list of all of the day to day responsibilities you had in the military. List the skills necessary to fulfill these responsibilities and any awards or decorations you have received for performing them. List them in the back of this guidelet. All members of the military have learned teamwork, leadership skills, personal reliability, honest accountability and a solid, full day's work ethic. Make this list personal to you and point this out to potential employers.

The Web, The Apps, The Internet -

NOTHING will be more important to you in your transition from the military to civilian life than your ability to utilize the Internet to search, educate, inform and publicize yourself, your skills, your availability. Internet access is essential <u>and it is as simple to access as your nearest public library or job center</u>. I cannot emphasize enough what an indispensable tool this is. If you do not own a personal computer, make plans to get one. Put it in your budget. There is never a need or an opportunity you can't access somewhere on the Web. If you don't know how to use one, LEARN. Take a class.

Again, your local library will most likely offer instruction. TAKE ADVANTAGE of this resource. Your life will be much easier with this knowledge.

A Few Things to Remember about Computers;

"Getting information off the Internet is like taking a drink from a fire hydrant."
-Mitchell Kapor

"Computers are good at following instructions, but not at reading your mind."
-Donald Kluth

"Computers are magnificent tools for the realization of or dreams, but no machine can replace the human spark of spirit, compassion, love and understanding."

-Louis Gerstner

"Never trust a computer you can't throw out a window."
-Steve Wozniak

Diplomas, Degrees, Certifications – Get them, copy them and distribute them. High school and college degrees can be obtained by contacting the school or, if necessary, the Board of Education in the town where you earned the degree. Certifications issued by a training agency can be obtained by contacting that agency, trade union or school. Have 'em, you'll need 'em.

These are important if you have gained a High School GED or a college degree while in the service. Also, any vocational certificates and documentation of any training programs you might have completed should be kept in a safe place. These will all help towards procuring a job, and in some cases, employers will hire you based on your experience. A successful military career speaks to an individual's integrity, an ability to work with and supervise others, and above all else a personal commitment to a job well done. If you have a prior degree or certificate, you will need to write to the school or college where you obtained it and request a copy.

Resource List - Many resource lists exist for veterans. You should put together a list of all the resources you find during your research. If you do not, there are many resources available through public libraries, employment offices and service organizations such as the American Legion, Veterans of Foreign Wars (VFW), Disabled American Veterans

(DAV) and others. More on service organizations later.

Normally, when you go to your local Social Services Office, they will have pamphlets and lists of resources for veterans looking for housing, employment and other services. Many facilities carry pamphlets you can look at that have resource lists on them. The bottom line is that if you are sincere about getting the help that you need; you will always be able to find resources and organizations that are willing to help. If you are willing to put the work in, most are more than willing to help. Nobody however, no service organization nor community resource should work harder than you to meet your employment or housing goals. And they should see that.

Resume - Some military branches offer the opportunity for you to attend a program in which you will create a resume and a discharge plan before being separated. If this was not the case for you, you should put together a professional-looking resume to send to potential employers.

Appendix A has a section for Resume Building and covers what a resume should look like and what it should include.

Short/Long Term Goals - You should write out a list of short and long-term goals for yourself.

This will provide something for you to work toward, and a sense of accomplishment when you set a long-term goal or obtain gainful employment within "one week" as a short-term goal. Do not set your aims too high, rather be realistic. If you are already living in a comfortable home or apartment, do not make one of your goals to "Own a house within six months." Be real about your goals. Eventually you will achieve them if you take your time and be patient.

Social Security Card - You should have this important card as part of your discharge packet. If not, you can get it yourself by writing to or visiting the Social Security Administration office in your town.

Voter Registration - If you want to reinstate your local voting rights as a citizen each state has different requirements. Some states will automatically restore your voting rights; other states require you to register or re-register to activate your voting privileges. **Do not skip this step.** Your vote is your voice, do not live silently. Research the state that you are in, and the state in which you may move to. Each state is different, and the state's regulations will be the ones followed. There is a federal mandate to restore your rights; individual states can and do make additional regulations. The system can be terribly slow in recognizing this, so please make sure you

have whatever paperwork necessary to instigate your voting rights. Register to VOTE. You cannot be heard without using your voice. Voting is one way to use your voice and be heard.

Time Management Plan - Let us face it, when you're discharged, you're going to find that either you just don't have enough time for the things you want to do or not enough time to do the things you **have to do**! Create a time management plan for yourself. It could be something like this:

If you have a Job	*And if you do not*
8:00am – Go to Work	6:30am – Wake up
4:00pm – Go Home	7:00am – . Breakfast
4:30pm – Dinner	7:30am – Job Search
5:30pm – Gym	12:00pm – Lunch
7:00pm – Socialize	12: 30pm– Job Search
9: 00pm –Home	5:00pm – Home Rest

Of course, these are examples, and your schedule will probably be different. But if you have a schedule, then you are much more organized and aware than someone who does not. Remember when you are out of work there are no weekends off. Your job search is your career search, it doesn't stop on Friday afternoon.

The Freedom of Information Act

(FOIA) - In the quest to obtain your necessary personal and vital documents, this law will make it easier to do so. Every citizen of the United States can secure documentation from the Federal Government if they are a part and parcel of the public domain, unless it will be an invasion of another person's privacy.

In addition, most, if not all states, have a Federal counterpart to this Act commonly called the Freedom of Information Law (FOIL). In most cases, any documents that are public in nature are accessible to the public, except as mentioned above--if the information invades the privacy of another.

Therefore, almost all documents relating to you personally are accessible to you, unless exempt by a specific section of the law. To prepare oneself for successful transition into the community, it is recommended that documents you do not have should be secured (see document checklist in next chapter).

If you do not have your documents or information that you will need get them or find out how to get them!!!!

CHAPTER 3
Transition Preparation

***Here are most, if not all the things you should be acquiring or think about prior to, or immediately after your discharge:

Think about these questions prior to your discharge date:

Where will you be staying?

_____

Who will you be staying with?

_____

Where will you be working?

_____

What programs or classes will you be attending?

_____

Who is your closest support person?

_____

Is all your paperwork in order? Check into it. What do you still need?

_____

Do you have a valid ID? Get it.

_____

Do you have transportation home? Get it.

Tip: Uber is a great alternative if you don't have your own transportation.

Document Checklist:

___ Birth Certificate
___ Credit Report
___ Daily routine / habits
___ Documents needed / Budget planning
___ Driver's License / Unpaid Tickets
___ Employment possibilities
___ Resume
___ Funding Sources
___ Housing possibilities
___ Medical records / Physical conditioning
___ Miscellaneous paperwork if any
___ Realistic goal planning
___ Social Security Card / Benefits printout
___ Time Management

Here are several considerations for some, not all, veterans about to be discharged:

___ Child Support
___ Classified ads / Job leads

___ Access to the internet (libraries, job centers, etc.)
___ Clothing
___ Do you have a phone?
___ Drug Counseling / AA / NA
___ Entertainment
___ Family visits
___ First day expenses
___ First day goals
___ First day thoughts
___ Identification
___ Legal Issues
___ Medical needs / Medicaid card / Medical Insurance
___ Memo book / Addresses / Phone Numbers / Contacts
___ Metro card
___ Place to live.
___ Resume package
___ Spiritual Support / Church / Mosque / Synagogue

Things to Watch Out For:

Now here are some things you will need to watch out for:

People - Those who know you are getting discharged do not always have your best interests at heart. They may think it is time to "celebrate." You have grown up a lot in the past few years. This may not necessarily be true for the friends you left behind. Consider carefully your companions. "Celebrate", you bet, but that doesn't mean get drunk or high enough to do something that can derail all your future plans.

If you associated with people who were immature or messing with drugs before you went into the military, you might think that now you're out that it's OK to be a part of that lifestyle again. Make new, better friends.

Places - If you do go back to the same neighborhood, you do not have to do the same things you were doing before you enlisted. You've grown up. A lot. If you live in a high-crime area, you will just have to be more diligent in staying away from the negativity.

Remember, going out to bars or nightclubs is normal, getting smashed drunk or stupid high is not! Hanging out with a group of people on the street who are dealing or using drugs, even if you are not involved, can easily drag you down. You are an Honorably Discharged United States Armed Forces Veteran. There is honor in that, there is honor in you. Drugs and alcohol are not going to enhance that honor.

33

Things - There are many things you should be wary of on the day of your discharge. You are now free to make all of your own decisions. Good ones, bad ones, smart ones, stupid ones. Choose wisely. Decide which things will make your life better in the long run. That new car may be bright and shiny but how much debt comes with it? Insurance costs? Gas mileage? Where do you park that beauty? You are in the "long run" now. Just because you can afford a toy doesn't mean you should buy a toy. You've got a life to run. Run it sensibly.

While in the military you are likely to have become comfortable around and carrying firearms. There are serious restrictions to firearm possession in the civilian world. Research these, know your rights and never abuse them. Do not assume that others are as comfortable as you around firearms. Discretion is the key word.

You are not the same person who left his home and his upbringing to join the military. You have been places, done things, accomplished much and become not only an adult, but as an honorably discharged veteran you are a valued member of our nation's most important fraternity. It now falls to you to respect yourself and your fellowship in that fraternity. **YOU MUST MAKE YOUR OWN FUTURE!**

CHAPTER 4
Getting on the Web & Where & Why

Your job hunt, your post-military career path, is the single most important issue you should concern yourself with. The time in your life has come to think "long game", to find employment which is meaningful (to you), lucrative, (that meets your financial needs and obligations), and secure (so that you can build the rest of your life around it).

Workshops and websites available through the Veterans Administration will be a crucial, essential part of your successful job hunt, and even more, your career path.

A great place to start is with the Veterans Administration's **Office of Transition and Economic Development (OTED)** and their **Transition Assistance Program.** There are two ways to access this program. First is by visiting your local Veterans Administration facility and asking to speak to a counselor within this department, and accessing their website (see Appendix C for list of Resources and associated links to websites).

BOOTS ON THE GROUND is always the best way to go. Be present. Make a personal connection. Interact. Sure, it's more difficult to get up and go, but the personal connection you may make will more than make up for the inconvenience of getting there.

If these in-person services are not available in your area go on-line to learn about the VA Transition Assistance Program (TAP) <u>tapevents.org</u> and begin your mission there. On this site you will find a series of on-line courses ranging from Employment Fundamentals to Career Transition. See Appendix C, Resources for more information.

These courses are lengthy, all-inclusive and essential for your success. Use them, watch them and take notes. This is all about you, your progress, your rights and your future.

Another web site offering lots of useful information, links, advice and support is <u>military.com</u> (more info found in Appendix C, Resources). Go there, click around. Take notes. Follow up. Be your own supervisor. Nobody should be more interested in your success than YOU.

EDUCATION OR EMPLOYMENT? If you had the foresight to establish an educational savings program while on active duty now is the time to utilize it. There are a host of factors which go into choosing an educational plan. Two year or four year college? Full or part time? Local or distant? What major to choose? Where to live while attending classes?

There are no generic answers to these questions. Do your research. Choose an institution which meets your educational goals, one that is within your financial reach. Once again many schools offer a veteran's preference for admission. The best way to find out all the answers here is to **VISIT** the college or trade school. **TALK** to an educational counselor. Find the Veterans Affairs office on campus. **SEEK OUT** any veteran's fraternities or organizations associated with the school. **Boots on the Ground**. There is no substitute.

If you have not accumulated any GI Bill Educational Savings while in the service check for additional assistance programs which may be available at the state or local level. On-line research is very helpful here, your local Veterans Administration offices and websites and independents such as militaryfamilies.com (see Appendix C for more info) have links and 800 numbers to follow this path.

Just a word about student loans. They are easy to obtain, quick cash. The debt, along with the interest payments which accrue are going to follow you for a long, long time in life. Get them if you need them, avoid them if you have alternatives such as part time work, work-study curriculum, or apprentice work days.

"If you are not willing to learn, no one can help you. If you are determined to learn, no one can stop you."

-**Zig Zigler**

"Education is the passport to the future, for tomorrow belongs to those who prepare for it today."

-**"Malcom X"**

"The value of a college education is not the learning of many facts. But the training of the mind to think."

-**Albert Einstein**

"The beautiful thing about learning is that no one can take it away from you"

-**BB King**

CHAPTER 5
An Example Discharge Program

Here is an example of a successful discharge program.

You should create your own discharge program at the end of this example. I suggest you use this as a template to guide you in the right direction. You do not have to do everything that is shown here. Just do what is relevant for you.

SHORT TERM

Week One:

1) Report and establish a positive relationship with the Veterans Administration.
2) Have a secure, safe living arrangement.
3) If necessary, go to the Department of Motor Vehicles (DMV). Verify and update your driver's license. Clear any violations.
4) Decide on education or employment. Start the hunt.
5) Visit the local service organizations such as the American Legion, VFW (Veterans of Foreign Wars), DAV (Disabled American Veterans). Inquire as to their programs and opportunities for members. Make contact.

6)   Open a local savings and checking account.

EMPLOYMENT

Week Two:

1)   Schedule an appointment with an employment office.
2)   Organize your clothing for job interviews.
3)   Get copies of your resume and cover letter.
4)   Go to the Department of Labor and request job search and employment assistance.
5)   Find and attend a social outlet, church group, athletic club. Time to make new friends, new social contacts.
6)   Get a job to hold you over until you can get one in your field.
7)   Find and attend outpatient support groups such as AA/NA if necessary.
8)   Follow up on unfinished tasks from week one.

FINANCIAL PLAN

Week Three:

1)   Every payday deposit a minimum of $10, if possible, into your saving account.
2)   Start using your checking account to pay bills and transfer money into your savings account.
3)   Begin to establish a line of credit by applying at a local retail outlet for a store credit card. Use

them once a month for 6 months. Pay the full balance to decrease monthly interest rates. This helps establish a positive credit history.
4) Continue to attend positive social activities.
5) Find and enjoy a hobby.

SOCIALIZATION & HEALTH

Week Four:

1) Focus and reinforce all my positive activities, make them habits, not obligations.
2) Consider independent living such as a small apartment with low rent.
3) Take note of your diet. Learn to eat healthy. Less junk food, less calories. Feel better, be better.
4) Continue working and saving money.
5) Attend outpatient daily or nightly AA/NA meetings if necessary.

90 DAYS AFTER DISCHARGE

1) Explore and apply for any Veterans Administration approved technical training or apprentice programs.
2) Decide which career you want to pursue.
3) Decide to attend full or part-time training. This will depend on the school schedule and financial

situation including how much money you have saved.

4) Continue attending outpatient daily or nightly AA/NA meetings if necessary.

5) Follow up on all job applications and contacts and log them.

6 MONTHS AFTER DISCHARGE

1) Review your finances. How much have you saved? What is the most productive use of this money?

2) Keep your focus and study in your part-time or full time vocational training.

3) Continue to work and pay your rent and bills.

4) Establish and maintain positive social activities. Make new friends, cherish old ones.

5) Plan a vacation, a getaway that is within your budget. You've earned it.

6) Continue attending outpatient daily or nightly AA/NA meetings and self-help programs if necessary.

1 YEAR AFTER DISCHARGE

1) Graduate from a college or vocational program.
2) Continue to seek full-time employment of a career.
3) Credit is established; I have buying power.
4) Increase weekly savings deposits as my career builds.
5) Continue attending outpatient daily or nightly AA/NA meetings and self-help programs.

LONG TERM GOALS

1) Continue attending outpatient daily or nightly AA/NA meetings and self-help programs.
2) Begin dating the right partner.
3) Start a family.
4) Find a home and begin a new chapter with a partner I love and a family.

****

A MAN OR WOMAN WITHOUT A PLAN IS ALREADY BEHIND IN LIFE
WITHOUT A PLAN OR GOALS,
YOU CANNOT
EXPECT TO SUCCEED
****

This is the conclusion of the first five chapters. The author has given you many important aspects of how to succeed when discharged. Without being honest with yourself, you might as well throw this guidelet away or give it to someone who is willing to take the necessary steps to succeed.

A person who continues to do the same things hoping for a different result is misled and destined for failure. Admit to yourself that you are engaging in an insane pursuit that will only lead to failure on the installment plan.

You should create a plan like the example on the previous pages. This will help you stay structured and you will know what to do and where to go next without having to always remember!

NOW is the time!

"A goal without a plan, is a wish."
-Doug Sanders

"If you don't have a plan, you become part of someone else's plan."
-Terrance McKenna

"There are dreamers and there are planners: the planners make their dreams come true."
-Troy Steven

"The sooner you start planning your life, the sooner you will live the life you dream of."
-Hans Glint

INTERLUDE I
The Greatest and The Most

Here is a little break from the important stuff. If you always try to live by these ideals, you should be fine:

The most destructive habit	**WORRY**
The greatest joy	**GIVING**
The greatest loss	**LOSS OF SELF-RESPECT**
The most satisfying work	**HELPING OTHERS**
The ugliest personality trait	**SELFISHNESS**

The most endangered species	**LEADERS**
Our greatest natural resource	**OUR YOUTH**
The Greatest "shot in the arm"	**ENCOURAGMENT**
The greatest problem to overcome	**FEAR**

The most effective sleeping pill	**PEACE OF MIND**
The most crippling failure	**EXCUSES**
The most powerful force in life	**CREATIVITY**
The most dangerous pariah	**A GOSSIP**

The World's most incredible computer
HUMAN BRAIN
The worst thing to be without   **HOPE**
The deadliest weapon   **THE TONGUE**
The two most powerful words   **"I CAN"**

The greatest asset   **FAITH**
The most worthless emotion   **SELF PITY**
The most beautiful attire   **A SMILE**

The most prized possession   **INTEGRITY**
The most powerful channel of communication
PRAYER
The most contagious spirit   **ENTHUSIASM**

Without heroes we are all plain people, and don't know how far we can go."

-**Bernard Malamud**

"My heroes are those who risk their lives every day to protect the world and make it a better place – Police, Firefighters and Members of the Armed Forces."

-**Sidney Sheldon**

"Our veterans accepted the responsibility to defend America and uphold our values when duty called."

-**Bill Shuster**

"Duty. Honor. Country. These three hallowed words reverently dictate what you ought to be, what you can be, what you will be."

-**General Douglas MacArthur**

INTERLUDE II
Holding onto Positive Energy (HOPE)

Hope is the belief in something not yet realized, but nonetheless stimulates our consciousness. We, of course, hope that we will become a success in life, but that does not mean that we can do nothing to foster that hope. Hope, you see, is associated with action.

Hope, Like Energy, is Dynamic

The will to live is rooted in action. If we hope that tomorrow, we will be alive to accomplish something or anything, it begins with our thoughts. How many times have we heard of people who have lost their hope to live when they were sick and not surprisingly, they die rather quickly?

On the other hand, there are those who are sick but have hope in living and many times get better simply due to that hope alone! This hope that we have is rooted in action (energy) of some unseen force. For many. It is a belief in a Creator or other benevolent Higher Power. Alcoholics Anonymous, and all other 12-step groups, dictate that we look to a Higher Power for hope in being sober or free from whatever addiction or habit that group addresses. In many seemingly hopeless cases, it works.

How many of us have heard people say that they hope to be happy in life, and they believe that money will bring them happiness? There are many rich people who are unhappy; it is a known fact. It is not that happy people live life differently than unhappy people, but the fact is that happy people view life differently. They have a conscious hope that life will be happy in some way for them. It frequently is happy- - much more so than for those that do not believe in hope.

When I say that I hope to live to be a hundred, and then don't do anything to help make that hope a reality, I probably will have a lot less of a chance to live to that ripe old age. If a person is fooling themselves like this, they cannot really believe in the hope that they have unless they are just mouthing the words.

Miserable people doing nothing to advance themselves and waiting to be saved or served say that they hope to change their lives, and do nothing to prepare themselves for that hope, then they are simply speaking empty words that in all actuality carry no hope at all. They will most likely remain miserable, floundering in their hopeless state.

The acronym **HOPE** stands for:

HOLDING ONTO POSITIVE ENERGY.

We can see the foundation of hope as not only something unseen, but also something you can help bring to life through positive action.

Home is where your heart is. Do not be fooled by the glitter of diamonds--even fake ones shine brightly! Depend on yourself. Emotions are poor masters but good servants. Do not allow your emotions to overrule your intelligence.

SOME HOPES AND DREAMS:

_____

_____

_____

_____

_____

If you can't name 'em, you won't have 'em.

BEGINNING OF PART II

Now you can actively take part in your successful transition to society, by filling in the blanks here in Part Two and putting down on paper your assets. You can prepare for the future and set yourself on the path to success. Without a good job, you will have difficulty "Living Well". Getting a good job that you enjoy will give you a great feeling of accomplishment, as well as allowing you to live well enough to enjoy life and purchase the things you like.

To get a good job, you'll need a good resume, and this part of the guidelet will help you with that and give you a few pointers on other things you should watch out for that might set you back on your road to success.

Earlier we pointed out that there is no substitute for **BOOTS ON THE GROUND** in your job search or social reentry. Let's add one more. **GET IT IN WRITING.** Whenever you apply for a position, visit a social or community help office, get a confirmation, in writing, of your visit whenever possible. Politely ask for an e-mail confirmation or follow up letter. Have your contact information readily available to make this as convenient as possible for the authority. Remember, "Verbal promises are not worth the paper they are written on." Sad, but often true. **GET IT IN WRITING!**

CHAPTER 6
Preparing for the First Day

The Most Important One!

Now you can create your own personal profile and success plan using this guidelet. This will help you get an idea of where you stand.

What are your objectives (plans) when discharged?

_____

_____

_____

What are your employment possibilities when discharged?

_____

_____

_____

List your Special Skills: (Everybody has them!)

_____

_____

_____

Family Status: ___Single ___Married _Divorced

Number of children (if any): _____

Child Support Amount: _____

The following are reminders. Please check them off if they apply to you and if you have not obtained these, start getting them now!! You will need these things upon discharge.

Have you obtained?

1. ___Assurance of employment?

2. ___A place to stay?

3. ___Programs to attend?

4. ___Address of a Mentor or Reference?

5. ___Suitable Clothing?

The Day of Discharge

Here are the things you will need to be concerned with on the day you are discharged:

1) Where will you be staying?

_____

2) Who will you be staying with?

_____

3) Where will you be working?

_____

4) What program(s)/support groups will you be attending?

_____

5) Where is your nearest Employment Opportunity?

_____

6) When are your first monthly payments due?

_____

7) Is all your paperwork in order? [ ] Y or [ ] N
If not, what else do you need?

_____

8) Do you have a valid ID? [ ] Y or [ ] N
If not, how and when will you get it?

_____

***These are things you need to address somewhere around the second day after your discharge, after you have had a day or so to get reacquainted with being out of the service:

Second Day... Things to Remember:

- Breakfast / Lunch / Dinner
- Daily review – Accomplishments – Plan for tomorrow
- Getting up and out – stay busy!
- Looking for employment – Filling out applications. **Boots on the ground!**
- Recording my movements and places visited
- Where am I going? What am I doing today?

***Here are things you should try to accomplish during the first week you are discharged, a few days after you have become somewhat comfortable with being out of the military:

First Week Goals

- Apartment
- Continuing Medical needs
- Family matters
- Food
- Getting a group and sponsor – AA/NA or other
- Getting a job
- Laundry
- Memo book recording. *Save everything!*
- Relationships
- Schooling
- Weekends – How will you handle them?

Remember, *do not overwhelm yourself!* These reminders and checkpoints are only here to tell you that these are the things you will have to be mindful of and go over before and after you are discharged. **Review them now!**

You have to make sure that you know about these things before you get out there because some people, especially those that have been out of circulation for a long time, don't know what they're getting into upon discharge. It is a changing world out there!

It is easy to have a daily schedule and have your life ruled by others while you are in the service. It is when you are discharged that you have to take charge and do all these things yourself. Few people and organizations will help you unless you are willing to help yourself.

Wish List

Make a list of a few personal rewards and pleasures you can work toward.

_____

_____

_____

_____

_____

CHAPTER 7
Finances & Living Well

Problems with money and the inability to budget income efficiently can be some of the more important factors a person who is trying to move ahead in his life may encounter.

These are things you will have to be aware of that you will be paying for when you get on your feet and start making money. Fill in those that apply to you:

MONTHLY REGULAR EXPENSES:

CHILD CARE / SUPPORT:	$_____
GROCERIES / FOOD:	$_____
HEALTH CARE:	
Medications:	$_____
Eye Care / Glasses:	$_____
Dental:	$_____
INSURANCE:	
Car:	$_____
Medical:	$_____
Life:	$_____
Home / Rental:	$_____
INTERNET COSTS (Necessity!)	$_____
RENT / MORTGAGE	$_____
SAVINGS	$_____

TAXES: $_____

TELEPHONE: $_____

CELL PHONE: $_____

TV / CABLE / INTERNET: $_____

TRANSPORTATION: $_____

OTHER: $_____

TOTAL MONTHLY REGULAR EXPENSES:

$_____

MONTHLY INFREQUENT EXPENSES:

Books Magazines/Reading Material: $_____

Clothing / Footwear: $_____

Cosmetics / Hygiene/ Personal Care: $_____

Credit Card Payments: $_____

Entertainment / Movies / Etc.: $_____

Gifts: $_____

Home Maintenance: $_____

Pet Food / Supplies: $_____

Restaurants: $_____

Vacation: $_____

Vehicle Expenses / Repairs / Gas / Tolls:

$_____

TOTAL MONTHLY INFREQUENT EXPENSES:

$_____

> **Tip: Do not save what is left after spending. Spend what is left after saving.** –Troy Steven

Notes:

_____

_____

_____

_____

_____

CHAPTER 8
Some Words on Employment

This is one of the most important issues among those restarting their civilian lives after the military. Frequently, a person is discharged having obtained important training while on active duty and finds that it is nearly impossible to find a job only because of his inability to translate those military skills into civilian understanding.

You will need to put together a good resume and showcase your military skills and demonstrate how they will apply to civilian employment.

A usable resume will allow you to better understand what you have to offer. DO NOT pad your resume. Be truthful. It will be the fastest way to lose the employment opportunity if someone asks you about what information you have given. Remember: the technology today can reveal the padding/ oversight within seconds of an employer's inquiry. Most employers hire a contracting company to verify the backgrounds of all potential employees; even before the interview is completed.

> **Tip: See Appendix A for detailed instructions on how to prepare a cover letter, resume, fill out job applications and obtain references.**

Honesty is the best policy *in this respect. With the onset of the terrorist attacks of 9/11/2001, a number of "services" have sprung up, (profitable ones of course), that make it very easy for a potential employer to look up a specific person and completely document their background. If your application contains fabrications or exaggerations, and if it shows up (and it will!), there is a good chance you will not be hired.*

Tip: Do a google search on yourself. You may be surprised how much information about you is on the Web, and if derogatory or too personal you may be able to remove it.

Remember that the format and information will change as the job markets change. The included sample application in Appendix A is a good worksheet to keep your information handy. Carry this with you to places of employment. Please note that most <u>all</u> applications will be completed online using computers (including state benefits, healthcare registration, etc.). They are tedious and taxing on patience. Be patient.

Yes, you do need computer skills to apply for most jobs and benefits. You also need an email account and address. Public libraries have free classes to learn the basics including keyboarding and typing (you need these to use a computer effectively). Employment centers and libraries have free computer time. Get a library card to access all this free information and great resources.

Resume's and cover letters need to have the words describing the job you are applying for included. For example, if the skill of "carpenter" is listed in the job advertisement, then make sure those exact words are in your resume and cover letter, so that if you are searching for a job as a carpenter on the computer and your resume states that you worked at "Mastercraft Woodworking" as a carpenter from 2010-2015, your skills will match the hiring managers' requirements, and you have a better chance of getting the job. Essentially, the computer is looking for "key words" from your resume to match the job description and skill set needed for the job. Use your online resources to review, download, and use current formats for resumes and cover letters. You do not have to pay for this service. It is online. It is free.

Tip: Have 2 people you trust review your resume for typos, sentence structure, and how effectively it outlines your skills and education.

Keep up with the latest using YOUR resources from Career Source Centers, Employment Offices, and Libraries.

Remind an employer that you can be federally bonded, and that your potential employer can potentially get a hefty tax break for hiring a veteran. Like YOU.

There are millions of companies out there that have veterans already in their employ. You CAN get a job, usually an incredibly good one, if you have done your homework and presented yourself honestly. Be persistent and have faith.

If you have saved some money or have family or others out there to back you, think of starting your OWN business. There are government loan programs set up to specifically fund veteran businesses. Research them. Write a business plan. Apply.

There are many businesses out there that hire ONLY veterans and many others certainly prefer and respect your military service. Let an employer know your military background and how your training can make you their ideal employee.

References:

Ask for and save reference letters from as many sources as you can. Your former sergeants, supervisors, commanding officers, neighbors and teachers, all are good sources for reference letters. Keep them with you along with copies of your DD-214 so they can be provided to a potential employer, upon request.

That is all there is to it! If you make your resume look professional, you will look professional as well. I suggest using Microsoft Word to create your resume, it is resident on most computers, as well as a good printer with quality resume paper. If you have the right skills for the job you are trying to get, you will have a good chance to get the kind of job you're looking for.

If you explain yourself honestly and convey to an employer your sincere desire to be a dependable employee, YOU WILL BE SUCCESSFUL.

Some more things to remember:

If you get a call from your prospective employer to appear for an interview: dress appropriately for the type of job you are applying for. If it is an office job, a suit and tie are usually required, and if it's a manual labor job of some type you should wear pressed pants (or jeans) and a clean, pressed shirt.

If you are nervous, try not to let your potential employer know it! Get to the point, and try to conduct yourself in a respectful, calm manner. Let your potential employer know you're bettering yourself in every way possible and have a sincere desire to settle down, work hard and be successful in life.

If you are hired, thank him or her, again, if you are honest and your demeanor reflects it, you will soon end up right where you want to be.

The reality is that you may end up putting in a hundred applications and all your college and military experience means nothing when you do not present it properly. What do you do?

One option: If you cannot find a job, think about volunteering somewhere. You would be amazed at the contacts that can be made when you volunteer.

Also, most states have some type of JOB link that offers free help in writing resumes, making copies, job listings, job hunting classes and computer classes, etc. If all else fails, think about the possibilities of starting your own business.

If you have not practiced keeping a good filing system, then you must begin to practice before you leave the service. Filing all your movements, conditions, purchases, job applications, etc. is especially important. If you cannot afford a filing cabinet get some good sturdy boxes and tall folders to which each item can be marked.

Having a personal filing system will also give your life more order – an important aspect of being successful in life.

Make a list of your skills / hobbies below that might interest a potential employer. If you don't have any, **GET SOME!**

Skills & Hobbies, Special Interests:

_____

_____

_____

_____

_____

Employers are not hiring only your qualifications. They are hiring YOU. Let the employer know who you are and what you can bring to their company.

CHAPTER 9
Service organizations

There are a host of service organizations out there. Being a veteran makes you part of a fraternity which runs deep in our culture. This fraternity is marked by differing clubs, chapters and lodges, each with its own set of traditions, requirements, benefits and advantages.

In most small towns across America veterans halls dot the landscape. The American legion, Veterans of Foreign Wars, Disabled American Veterans, National Veterans Foundation, AMVETS, Paralyzed Veterans of America, Military Order of the Purple Heart, Iraq & Afghanistan Veterans of America, Student Veterans of America, National Association of Black Veterans are just a few from a very long list. Each has a website. Their websites have links. See Appendix C for a list of available resources and links to their websites.

FIND THEM. FOLLOW THEM. USE THEM.

Most importantly, **VISIT THEM**. Many of these organizations are made up of older veterans, more experienced veterans and helpful, community oriented veterans. Get to know them and Allow them to get to know you.

If you are on a job hunt, let them know. Bring resumes.

BOOTS ON THE GROUND

You will need some documentation to join these organizations and reap their benefits. Have these with you when you visit.

Your DD-214 is essential. Have copies. Leave copies. If you are applying at the Disabled Veterans of America (DAV), Wounded Warrior Project, or Purple Heart Association facilities, have the appropriate medical documentation with you.

Nationwide there are upward of twelve thousand American Legion Posts with around two million members.

The Veterans of Foreign Wars has over six thousand posts with one and half million members.

The Disabled American Veterans Organization has thirteen hundred posts with over a million members.

These organizations are there for you. Use them. You have earned a welcome among them. I have listed only the top three, by membership, of the many veteran organizations in our country. Seek out the others. You must find them. They will not find you.

Many of these organizations have dues, annual or lifetime. If you are strapped for cash, ask if these fees can be waived or delayed until you find work.

DISCOUNTS, BENNIES, FREEBIES

There are literally **hundreds** of retail and professional services which offer generous discounts to veterans. Research them, look for their ads, ASK before purchasing. You will be surprised at how many outlets offer this benefit.

Here are a few:

- Lowe's & Home Depot Hardware Stores
- Verizon Wireless
- AT&T
- Sam's Club & Costco
- Almost All Car Rental Companies
- Under Armour Clothing
- CVS Pharmacy
- Dollar General Stores
- Office Depot & Office Max

These are but a few. Many restaurants, airlines and health services also offer veterans a discount on their services. Seek and you will find. Ask and you will receive.

RESOURCE LIST

IMPORTANT PHONE NUMBERS

CHAPTER 10
HOME SWEET HOME

How many of us have said--throughout the time we served-that we cannot wait until we get home. For many home means the house you grew up in, your family home. A great place to start, to begin the process of having a home of your own.

Here are a few facts and guidelines regarding another of your most important veteran's benefits - **the VA Home loan.**

First, who is eligible? All honorably discharged veterans may apply for a VA Home Loan. But this is NOT an automatic process. While the VA does not require a minimum credit score, most lenders do. The majority set a 640 minimum credit score. Some may offer 620. This is another reason to monitor and nurture your credit score as outlined earlier in this guide.

You VA home loan is a wonderful thing. Owning your own home can change your life, building equity, forcing savings, establishing stability. The process is complicated however and there is not enough room in this guidelet to walk you through the steps. The good news is that there are plenty of experts out there who will.

Realtors, want to sell you a house. If possible find a veteran relator. He or she will know the ropes. Before beginning the process of searching for a home, sit down with your bank or credit union loan officer. Find out what you can afford, learn how to budget the maze of closing costs, inspection reports, tax requirements, HOA's and moving expenses you will encounter. Once again there are experts out there to help with this process. Let them do the figuring, let them iron out the wrinkles, just make sure you completely understand each step of the process. Buying a home is only the first step, maintaining and living comfortably in your new home is up to you.

REMEMBER: EVEN THOUGH YOU HAVE LEARNED MANY THINGS DURING YOUR MILITARY SERVICE, IT MUST INCLUDE WHAT YOU HAVE LEARNED ABOUT YOUR-SELF. ASK YOURSELF AND REFLECT ON THESE QUESTIONS:

WHERE DO I WANT TO BE IN ONE YEAR?

_____
_____
_____

HOW AM I GOING TO GET THERE?

_____
_____
_____

Repeat this exercise for the coming years. You will find this incredibly useful. You can't hit a target you don't aim at.

WHERE DO I WANT OF BE IN FIVE YEARS?

_____
_____
_____

HOW AM I GOING TO GET THERE?

_____
_____
_____

No one is in charge of your future except you. You have demonstrated, by your honorable military service that you can set goals and attain them. There is little you will encounter in civilian life that you cannot overcome by using the same skills and perseverance you demonstrated during your military service.

"Twenty years from now you will be more disappointed by the things you didn't do than the things you did do. So throw off the bowlines. Sail away from safe harbor. Catch the trade winds in your sails. Explore. Dream. Discover." -Mark Twain.

CHAPTER 11
Conclusion

Remember, you are an **Honorable Discharged Veteran of the Unites States Armed Forces**. Like the many thousand before you your service has earned you respect, dignity and privilege. Veteran's benefits are not gifts. They are not handouts. You have earned them with your service.

If you have a solid commitment to your successful transition to a civilian career, you can do it, as long as you always remember where you are, what you're doing and who you're doing it with. There are benefits out there, lots of them. There are exemptions, waivers, incentives and subsidies, but it is up to you to find them, to utilize them properly, to prosper with them. **Do not wait for them to come to you. Do not expect any benefits counselor to work harder at your success than you are doing for yourself.** Do more, show more. Nothing you are likely to encounter in your transition to civilian life is going to be anywhere near as daunting as Basic Training, overseas deployments, the hazards you faced to life and limb in the military.

Take control of the rest of your life. NOW*!!*

APPENDIX A
Cover Letter, Resume,
Job Application, & References

Cover Letter

Wondering what to include in your cover letter? It is a good idea to include key points about why you are a great fit for the company and the best choice for the specific job. Of course, do not forget to ask for the interview—but keep it brief!

A cover letter should not read like a novel, no matter how great a plot you have. Remember to THANK the person for reviewing your qualifications and FOLLOW-UP with a thank you note, or e-mail once interviewed. (If you do not hear anything, follow-up in two days, if no response, move on. Companies are not letting the candidates know unless they are directly interviewing).

Again **BOOTS ON THE GROUND** is the absolute best way to apply for any position. Be there. Get noticed. Shake hands. Follow through.

Here is an example of a brief cover letter. Change or modify it as you wish. Make it yours.

John Smith   January 3, 2022
100 Main Street
Anytown, Alaska 12345
Tel: 123-456-7890

Re: Job Position Title and reference # / Job ID # (if applicable)

Dear Sir or Madam,

I am interested in applying for a position in your company. I have attached my resume and contact information and will make myself available for an interview at your convenience.

I have recently been honorably discharged from the Armed Forces and am interested in starting my civilian career with your organization. I can bring to your company a host of skills I utilized in my military service such as dependability, willingness to accept responsibility and self-motivation. Please consider me for any relevant position you may have. Thank you for taking the time to review my application.

Sincerely,
[Your Name] (Remember to sign if submitting this to a person or directly to company in paper format if not, print your name with computer as signature).

A Sample Resume

John Smith
100 Main Street
Anytown, Alaska 12345
Tel: 123-456-7890
E-mail: Smithjohn@yahoo.com

Skills
[Use this area to match the skills in the advertisement for the job] – remember to update resume for EACH job application – make sure to use the words in the advertisement for each job you are applying to – yes, a new resume & cover letter for EVERY job you want.

Experience
[This is the place for a brief summary of your key responsibilities and most stellar accomplishments.] – Use the key words in the job description to match the most relevant skills per position.

Education
[School Name, City, State] (Even if GED or a specific grade level).

[Major] (If no major, then do not include).

[Certificates of Vocational Education] (name of certificate, issuing institution – may need explanation of skills used during certifying process if confusing).

[ALL military training completed.] Your MOS duties. Rank at discharge. Decorations and awards.

[Certificates of Completion] (name and institution).

Volunteer Experience (additional skills not noted above – computer software/hardware or repair of something skills providing Added Value for Employer).

Outline this area with dates and time and contacts for the organizations you have volunteered for or provided services to -- use experience section to guide the formatting.

Job Application Form Sample:

***Use this as a guide – most applications are online only & you will need ALL this information to complete applications – be prepared to have all years of employment history available – just in case.

Instructions: Print clearly in black or blue ink. Answer all questions. Sign and date the form.

Personal Information

First Name
_____

Middle Name
_____

Last Name
_____

Street Address
_____

City, State, Zip Code
_____

Phone Number (___)
_____

Email
_____

_____

Have you ever applied to / worked for Company before? [ ] Y or [ ] N
If yes, please explain (include date):

_____

Do you have any friends, relatives, or acquaintances working for Company? [ ] Y or [ ] N

If yes, state name & relationship:

_____

If hired, would you have transportation to/from work? [ ] Y or [ ] N

Are you over the age of 18? [ ] Y or [ ] N

If you are under age 18, do you have an employment/age certificate? [ ] Y or [ ] N

If hired, would you be able to present evidence of your U.S. citizenship or proof of your legal right to work in the United States? [ ] Y or [ ] N

Have you been convicted of or pleaded no contest to a felony within the last five years? [ ] Y or [ ] N

If yes, please describe the crime - state nature of the crime(s), when and where convicted and disposition of the case.

_____
_____
_____

If hired, are you willing to submit to and pass a controlled substance test? [ ] Y or [ ] N

Position and Availability:

Position Applied For:

_____

Salary desired:
$_____

Are you applying for:

Temporary work – such as summer or holiday work?
[ ] Y or [ ] N

Regular part-time work? [ ] Y or [ ] N

Regular full-time work? [ ] Y or [ ] N

Days/Hours Available
Monday   _____
Tuesday   _____
Wednesday   _____
Thursday   _____
Friday   _____
Saturday   _____
Sunday   _____
Hours Available: from _____ to _____

If applying for temporary work, when will you be available?

_____

If hired, on what date can you start working?
___ / ___ / ___

Can you work on the weekends? [ ] Y or [ ] N

Can you work evenings? [ ] Y or [ ] N

Are you available to work overtime? [ ] Y or [ ] N

Are you able to perform the essential functions of the job for which you are applying, with / without reasonable accommodation? [ ] Y or [ ] N

If no, describe the functions that cannot be performed:

_____

Education, Training and Experience

High School
School name:

_____

School city, state, zip:

_____

Number of years completed:

_____

Did you graduate? [ ] Y or [ ] N

Degree / diploma earned:

_____

College / University:

School name:

_____

School city, state, zip:

_____

Number of years completed:

_____

Did you graduate? [ ] Y or [ ] N

Degree / diploma earned:

_____

Vocational School:

School Name:

_____

School city, state, zip:

_____

Number of years completed:

_____

Did you graduate? [ ] Y or [ ] N
Degree / diploma earned:

_____

Military:

Branch: _____

Rank in Military: _____

Total Years of Service: _____

Skills/duties:

_____
_____
_____
_____

Related details:

_____
_____
_____

APPENDIX B
Work Search Record

Keep a running list of potential employers, and the status of each job you applied for. If you interview with a company, be sure to get the name and phone number of the hiring manager, and the human resources contact. Follow up with them in a week or so if the job is a good fit and it is a company you want to work for. Remember talking to someone in person (**Boots on the Ground**) is the most effective.

Company Name:

_____

Company Location (City, State):

_____
_____

Position applied for:

_____

How did you hear about the job?

_____

Contact Method and date (Applied onsite, dropped off resume, Phone call, online application, sent email):

_____

Hiring Manager (Name, Phone #, email):

_____

Human Resources Contact (Name Phone # email):

_____

Additional Contact: (Name, Phone #, email):

_____

Phone Interview date:

_____

On-Site Interview date:

_____

Actions to take next (include follow up date):

_____

APPENDIX C Resources

VA Transition Assistance Program (TAP): On this site you will find a series of on-line courses ranging from Employment Fundamentals to Career Transition
tapevents.org

The National Veterans Foundation: provides live veteran counselors through online chat or their 888-777-4443 hotline or
http://www.nvf.org/

Veterans Administration's Office of Transition and Economic Development (OTED) and their **Transition Assistance Program:**
Google to find contact info.

Military.com: is another web site offering lots of useful information, links, advice and support is. Go there, click around. Take notes. Follow up. Be your own supervisor. Nobody should be more interested in your success than YOU.
military.com

The American Veterans and Service members Survival Guide: *How to Cut Through the Bureaucracy and Get What You Need – And are Entitled To* is an eBook published by Veterans For America available online at-
http://www.nvsp.org/images/Survival%20Guide-102309.pdf.

Militaryfamilies.com: An excellent source for varied veteran resources and social networking is available online at
militaryfamilies.com

The National Resource Directory (NRD): Available at -
https://www.nationalresourcedirectory.gov/.

Emergency housing assistance can be accessed at 1-877-424-3838 or by their website:
http://www.va.gov/HOMELESS/HUD-VASH.asp

Tip: Keep in touch with your service buddies, many of your struggles may be theirs and your successes may help them. Don't lose these connections.
Friends over Gold.

If you enjoyed this guidelet and find it useful, please take a few moments to write a review on your favorite store, and please refer it to anyone you know that may benefit from the information inside.

NOTES:

Made in the USA
Las Vegas, NV
26 September 2021

31172232R00056